# The Book
# Of Light

# The Book
# Of Light

David Matthew Brown

BOOKS

Winchester, UK
Washington, USA

First published by O-Books, 2012
O-Books is an imprint of John Hunt Publishing Ltd., Laurel House, Station Approach,
Alresford, Hants, SO24 9JH, UK
office1@jhpbooks.net
www.johnhuntpublishing.com

For distributor details and how to order please visit the 'Ordering' section on our website.

ISBN: 978 1 78099 664 6

Design: Stuart Davies


Printed and bound by CPI Group (UK) Ltd, Croydon, CR0 4YY

# CONTENTS

To my daughter Harper
You are loved

"The Great dawn is upon us, children of light, do not be frightened by the sight, come, just come, with your tired self, rest now in my arms sweet children."
**The Great Mother**

"All are equal in the light. No one should feel abandoned, scared, or lonely in my presence. The light I shine shines on all."
**The Great Sun**

# Forword

## by Emmanuel Dagher

Having known David for many years now, I find myself consistently inspired by the love and kindness he exudes with everyone he meets. The combination of his wisdom, strength, honesty, and sensitivity sets a precedent for the new blueprint that we are all becoming.

I met David when I was only a teenager, starry eyed & ready to delve into a more conscious way of being. It all started when my mom connected with David at a mind/body/spirit type of festival where he came to her booth and they instantly hit it off. He then invited her to attend one of his special meditation events. My mom insisted that I go with her to meet her new friend & see how 'awesome' he was. So, I did & from the moment I walked into the room, I knew that I was 'home' after feeling into the vibration of love that was set by David & the group of people he was speaking to.

David has a gift of taking spiritual principles that often seem a bit challenging to comprehend and simplifies them in way that makes it easy for anyone to understand. This to me is a form of alchemy, and I see David as a true Alchemist of spirituality. I've personally come to realize that it's in the most simple of things where the most profound miracles reside, and David was able to confirm this for me through his abilities & gifts.

Now, you as the reader have the opportunity to also experience David's insights & gifts for yourself. After reading this book, I noticed that much of what I took away from it was not so much just in the words, but rather the energy in between the words that I personally feel have the power to instantly transform one's life wherever they are in their journey.

It's a deep honor for me to know a luminous light like David, and to be able to call him my friend & brother.

With gratitude,

Emmanuel Dagher
Transformation Specialist, Spiritual Teacher, & Holistic Health Practitioner

# Authors Notes

I have had the incredible journey of working with many people. *The Book Of Light* is that journey. This book is not channeled. The style of the book is unique, maybe because early on in my writing career, I wrote tons of poetry. I love abstract work, writings, art, and as a creative being it makes sense to me to write in a somewhat non-linear style.

*The Book Of Light* is a book that you can read through, take time with, meditate, contemplate, and read through again. This book is for anyone and is a gentle reminder of who we are.

As always this book would not be possible without the wonderful work of Julie Anne Bruff. I shared my work with Julie and after reading the book she had lots of questions. I am glad I shared it with her and my heartfelt thanks to her keen eye.

I would like to thank John Hunt publishing and Moon Books for saying YES. As many of you know, having a child is very inspiring; my daughter Harper continues to inspire me. To my parents whose support and love is beyond words. To my sister Kathleen who has encouraged, supported, and cheered me on. And finally, to my support group of friends: Korena, Phoenix, Success Brannon, Rose Jabbour, John Gloria, and Julie, thank you.

Peace be with you
David Matthew Brown

# PART 1

The Book Of Story

1. There is only light. We are light. This is the truth, foundation, and beginning of everything.

2. Light emanates from one source.

3. It has no division and so it cannot be divided.

4. The source of the light is immense. It is everywhere and in all places at once.

5. There is no place the light is not.

6. So as Light, each is whole, perfect, complete, and constantly radiating this fullness. This is reality. This is nature and natural.

7. Light has no separation from itself, yet there appears to be separation. The appearance seems very real although it is false. The false is the story that appears to be real. Light has no sense of the story because the story is false.

8. The story is based on experiences proclaiming to be who the light is. The light is not the experience. If the light is looking to be an experience then it will feel lost amid the experience.

9. A story has a beginning, middle, and end. The story changes with the identity. For example if the light identifies with light then the experience can only be light. If the light indentifies solely with the storyteller then the experience will be heavy or light depending on how much the story is told, believed, and repeated.

10. When the storyteller is not observed, it takes the part of the foolish one and when this happens the storyteller is a foolish

storyteller and lives in a foolish kingdom. The foolishness that is described here is one in which the fool lacks instruction. A wise queen known as the heart; instructs and understands the nature of the storyteller.

11.   The foolish storyteller is filled with tantrums, rage, and lashes out. Whereas the wise queen is quiet, still, and filled with wisdom. Wisdom understands that truth does not come in loud voices. But truth is firm and does not change from moment to moment.

12.   The foolish storyteller is drunk on the ways of the world. Caught up in everything and everyone around it. Completely lost in story and the story is a translation.

13.   Wisdom is light understood.

14.   The queen is wisdom and she understands that she alone does not lead the children of the land. Her instructions come to her in stillness. There she simply listens in. As she listens, she becomes recharged by the stillness, invigorated, and alive. Her instructions always come from one source. The source is the one light. This is the truth, which is impersonal, and personal.

15.   The queen is not concerned with the world's problems; she is focused inwardly on the light. Her focus on the light is like an archer looking at a bull's eye, this focus allows her the freedom to observe and not be caught in the storyteller. She then can see the whole picture clearly and listen with an open heart. Then she will have the right solution for the world.

16.   The one caught up in the storyteller believes in everything

it is telling it. The storyteller is always sneaky. Sometimes it makes wonderful suggestions about others. It does this through comparing and competing. How tricky the foolish storyteller can be.

17. The queen has played this game many times, before her wisdom was attained. She now knows that truth (Light) never moves, wavers, doubts, or is confused. In fact she realizes it is always present. Heaven is now and there is no hell to believe in. Hell is the story.

18. Light is acceptance of everything as is.

19. In light all is neutral. Neutrality doesn't exist if the story-teller is allowed to have free range. Then everything becomes charged up. Good or bad, great or not so great, life and death, and the list goes on. Remember the queen under-stands that light has no division. That understanding allows her great strength.

20. The foolish storyteller sees the world as real, without asking, how can something that appears to be real, always be changing?

21. The Foolish storyteller needs everything to be the same in order for the story to be effective, yet the world is images appearing on the screen of the observer. If the observer gets caught up with the image then it is lost and needs the image to be something it simply can't be. It is being what it can be now.

22. The queen knows that the images come and go. She under-stands life as light. Nothing can be held on too, because there is nothing here. One cannot hold on to the breath.

23. A belief is something false. The belief needs a story for it to work. So it gains its story through experiences that it is identified with that brought forth a positive charge or negative charge in reaction to the identity it was carrying around at that time. Remember in truth there is only light. We are light.

24. The queen told a story to her disciples. She said, "A man was begging to understand why his life was lacking. The man went first to a holy man, " Why do I lack, I work hard, I am good, and honest." The holy man listened to the man, then said, "It will be paid to you my son in heaven." He was unsatisfied by the response, so he continued on his travels, he came across children who were playing. He observed how much fun they were having, so he asked them, "Children you are so full of life, "why do I lack, I work hard, I am good, and honest." The children laughed and the girl spoke, "You lack compared to what? You are good compared to what? You're honest compared to what?" Then the boy chimed in, "Sir you are none of those things." If you have ears to hear this then you have heard the truth.

25. A queen sees a foolish storyteller for what it is, a glutton, sloth, agitated, fragile, dramatic, and chaos ridden.

26. All must travel through the foolish storyteller. All must get caught up in it. All must.

27. Beware of the story. Question it. Until there is no more to question and there is only deep peace.

28. Observe the foolish ways of the storyteller.

29. Observe the folly of the storyteller.

30. Observe the beginning, middle, and end of the storyteller.

31. A disciple asked the queen, "Where did the foolish storyteller come from?" The queen responded, "Perhaps the better question is where does light come from?"

32. Discovering the light is a personal journey that everyone will make sometime.

33. The foolish storyteller doesn't want to be found out.

34. Light wants to be found. It wants to be discovered. Like a woman fishing in calm lake, she casts out her line, and sits patiently. Soon amid the peaceful lake she gets a bite. This is called inspiration. Inspiration is how light loves itself.

35. Light inspires, uplifts, and loves. That is its only nature.

36. The foolish storyteller is weighed down with memories, daydreams, dreams, beliefs, could've, should've, and judgment's. It's identified with the past, future, or what it needs. It negates all that is happening now.

37. A Disciple asked, "But mother queen when we talk with others, we tell them our stories, we tell them of our experiences, that is how we communicate with each other." The queen smiled, "Yes but you understand none of that is who you are, they are just experiences. Nothing more, nothing less."

38. The foolish storyteller is heavy. It has identified with everything outside itself. It feels empty and alone.

39. The queen listens only to the light. Because she is wise, her

desire is to lead with wisdom. Because she is no longer attached to the foolish one, she is light filled. Her hunger has gone. Her body is light.

40. When observing the foolish storyteller, just observe it.

41. Wisdom is only concerned with light; it could care less of the story.

42. The foolish storyteller creates a courtroom. Before it enters the court, the storyteller constructs a story of what may happen or has happened before. It is always on defense for the next the move. It doesn't trust anyone, let alone itself. In fact it is scared of its own stories. It constructs a judge, lawyer, and jury. The storyteller becomes all of them in every experience. Sometimes it sends the other person to jail for life, sometimes it lets them go, sometimes it belittles, gossips, brings evidence to the court on the person's guilt, or even in some cases puts the person to death. The queen of wisdom approaches every moment as it is. She deals with things as they are. She responds accordingly with no story attached.

43. The foolish storyteller wants to wake up. Wake up from what? The waking up is just another story to tell. Anything to be accepted, it doesn't like to be not accepted. That is when it's at its best storytelling, when nobody likes it, or everyone loves it.

44. The queen doesn't care about waking up, it is light. It doesn't care if others want to wake up or not. Foolish ones don't like instructions. The queen knows it takes instructions to find the light. She knows the foolish storyteller doesn't like simplicity it likes complexity. It wants steps

from here to  there, it wants to create challenges to get through, it needs to resist so it can create more problems, the more problems the better. It cannot accept now, if it did it would perish. The queen knows by being with the thought and feeling of fear, without wanting to change it, will bring about aliveness and transform the experience back to light. She understands that thoughts create feelings and chooses to call them thought feelings.

45. Many have come to the gate of light, and turned away and ran because their stories were too important to end.

46. Death does not exist. But it does exist in the story. Identity must have a beginning. "I" is the beginning and end.

47. The world is always changing on the screen of the observer.

48. Light never changes.

49. The world is lost in a foolish story that has a beginning, middle, and end. And in an attempt to create a new story, it replicates the old, because that is what it knows.

50. Fright doesn't exist in light. Story is frightening. And yes the story is frightening when it seems like all is great too. Because underneath the story of great is a sense of losing this greatness. And so the story continues to be great sometimes and not so great sometimes, both of which are thought feelings of what the foolish storyteller thinks is going on. Lost in translation is the story of life. Life has no story. Light is everything and so everything is good.

51. Everyone is coming back into light.

52. Light is everywhere and in all places but first must be discovered inside each person.

53. The foolish storyteller changes.

54. The foolish storyteller is identified with its jobs, health, relationships, schooling, money, family, parents, friends, and the story itself of the identities it created. Turning to the light is the process of losing the identity of trying to be this something in the world and coming back into nothing. Nothing is everything and everything comes from nothing.

55. The queen is light and understands that she is not identified with any part of the story. She needs, expects, and demands nothing from anybody at any time.

56. The foolish storyteller is caught up in the changeable and runs from the changeless.

57. Observe the runner and it stops. Observe the reaction and it goes away. Become the observed and the story will go away.

58. A disciple asked, "Dear queen why do we have the story?" The queen gently reminds the young disciple, "Why am I scared to be alone? Without answering this question thoroughly, you will only have the story. When you find the answer to this, you will find the cause of all your troubles, and you will discover the light that you are."

59. Questions are very helpful to the sincere.

60. You must be sincere in heart, to enter the light.

61. Most foolish storytellers just want answers, knowledge, to

be fixed now; they can't seem to handle the truth. A foolish storyteller wants Intel and uses Intel to gather information. The gathering of information is called intellect. Intellect is a sign of defense and brings about war. Intellect is not intelligence.

62. Observe the story as it is being told. Who is observing the story? What is observing? Where is the story coming from?

63. Turn away from the story, look away from the world, and allow the presence to be.

64. The fool lacks presence.

65. Don't be interested in the story just observe it.

66. The foolish Storyteller finds comfort in the noise. It needs noise, it needs a party to attend, it needs company, and yet wisdom needs stillness.

67. The queen turned to her disciples and explained, "Once the story is gone, you can begin to understand these books. They are the foundation of wisdom." She laid them on the table, the book of Heart, Innocence, Play, Stillness, and the Origins of Light.

# PART 2

## The Book of Heart

1.   The heart is a continuous beginning.

2.   Since there is only a beginning, there can be no end.

3.   Therefore the heart is the generator of now.

4.   The heart has no idea, image, of this thing called love. It in fact has no conditions, precepts, or how to be. It is the all and everything at once.

5.   Miracles are found in the discovery of the heart. The heart from the moment it came into life, only knows acceptance and unconditional giving. It takes action based only in the now.

6.   The heart is reality. It thinks only with nature. Sit in nature and you will discover the heart.

7.   The heart is the seat of the soul. It dictates to the mind what to do. The mind never dictates to the heart. If the mind tries to dictate to the heart, then struggle, and pain come. If the heart is still not being heard, it will continue to allow the foolish storyteller to lead, until the storyteller bows to the queen heart. Strong storytellers appear to be very willful and do not want to bow to the heart. A reminder that struggle and pain is simply lack of understanding the nature of the storyteller.

8.   Being open hearted is different from being hurt. Every mission is to become open hearted, not hurt. Repeating this again, every mission of every soul is to become open hearted. Being open hearted is life giving and receiving. Being hurt is holding on to everything, greed is hurt, selfishness is hurt, pain is hurt, struggle is hurt, hurt is

found in the storyteller. Continuing in other realms of hurt such is the case in lack, limitation, with holding, lying, cheating, all which the storyteller if not tamed to the queen heart will continue on until tamed by her. To be tamed by the queen heart is to bring understanding to the aspect called the unknown. If the student thinks it is lacking in anyway, it comes to the master for guidance. A good master is patient, aware, and firm, like the queen heart. It understands the nature of the student's journey, but it also knows the dangers and adventures. The master is both patient and firm. A parent does not let a child out of its sight for a moment. The parent is alert, alive, and present. Rather than punishing the child, a loving master brings patience and awareness to the situation, which brings forth understanding and leadership. The lion in the jungle is a heartfelt leader. It spends time in stillness and moves when it needs too. Storyteller is always trying to convince you that now is scary, frightening, or this world is against you.

9.   Dreams do not exist in the heart. Dreams exist in the student's mind. The heart has desire, not want. The heart desire can only be heard when attention is put on it, and taken away from the storyteller. The storyteller is here to dream, the heart is here to create and lead. The storyteller loves competition.

10.  In order to find the heart, one must discover all the conditions for which the heart is not. This is where forgiveness happens. To first acknowledge the error. The error is the storyteller. Because the student didn't trust the heart, it translated a story of what may have happened, should happen, or didn't happen. Expectations and demands are selfish aspects of the storyteller.

11. The heart moves moment to moment. The storyteller wanders everywhere. Yet it is teachable, it wants to be taught, used correctly, and understood.

12. Heart has no stories about love, because it is. It only knows complete acceptance of everything.

13. The heart understands what the storyteller is troubled over.

14. The heart is open, unless the storyteller is in control, then the heart appears to be closed for a brief time, or up until the heart takes over the journey. But this appearance of the heart closing is not the truth.

15. Awareness is the compass of the soul.

16. To be in the heart is a process. One cannot jump from storyteller to master. Rare occasions have allowed this to happen.

17. The heart is discovered in the awareness of the storyteller. When one can observe the storyteller without trying to change it, fix it, follow it, or tame it, then miracles come. It would be like riding a wild horse. Before you get on the horse, you observe it; let it be wild, aggressive, impatient, and impulsive. Then once you understand the horse, you can begin to tame it accordingly. The same is true with the heart. But first it allows the storyteller to run, be scared, and create fear. The heart allows this to happen, as to build a union with the storyteller. Every union goes through this process. Be afraid, scared, run, make up excuses, before it finally gives up. Awareness accepts life where it is. The heart is awareness, so it accepts the storyteller right where it is, because it knows all it needs to know, and that is enough.

18.   The heart is a miracle.

19.   The heart dances with what is; it can never be scared because it never creates anything against itself. The student mind does that. Once the students mind is seen for what it really is, then the stories will fall and the foundation will be made.

20.   Gentle Reminder: Stories do not exist in the heart.

21.   The heart moves freely, effortlessly, and gracefully.

22.   Since the heart has only a continuous beginning then it holds on to nothing. The storyteller cannot believe this at first because it is so captivated by its own story it resists this as a notion. Secondly, the storyteller needs another belief before it lets go of another. The storyteller would feel better with another story than the truth. The storyteller likes the extraordinary and resists the ordinary.

23.   The storyteller needs to dwell, think, hold on too, remember, demand, expect, look back, look forward, look out, look in, and create problems to over come. It does this to maintain its story. All of which will crumble when the heart takes over.

24.   The heart knows no problem, struggle, or heartbreak. Heartbreak should be called head break. The storyteller gets upset when it is not liked, not heard, not looked at, not seen, not loved, when something ends, and is addicted to not moving on. It loves to recreate what happened, bringing up stories, all which have been explained in book 1.

25.   The heart is free. All conditions are made up in the mind.

26. The storyteller cannot heal, it knows nothing of itself, for once it knows itself it ends the misery, and goes back to nothingness. Awareness is the way in which this process happens.

27. The heart is a healer and healing.

28. Once the heart is aware of itself, it magnetizes nothing but itself to it with effortless ease. Till that point, everything is used to bring it back to itself. The paradox of the storyteller is to help the heart achieve oneness. Waking up the heart to its nature, which is selfless. Till then the storyteller will live selfishly.

29. The mind is a dreamer of dreams. Dreams do not exist in reality.

30. The heart awakens everything, like a rose. The rose gives its scent to everyone. The sunlight lights everyone. Nature is for everyone. Love is natural.

31. A bird sings it songs from only one place and one place only, the heart.

32. Since the heart holds on to nothing, it recognizes that the storyteller creates conflict, since the heart is the master; it sees the lie for the lie. Awareness is aware of the lie, but doesn't change it, fix it, or deny it. It allows the lie to hear itself, when the lie is heard, change happens. The heart doesn't put the storyteller down, nor does it let the liar get away with it. The heart brings justice to the lie, by first acknowledging the lie, second bringing understanding to it, and third forgiving the liar.

33. There is nothing the heart doesn't know that is not known. The heart knows all and yet knows nothing at the same time this is called the presence. Masters know this.

34. The heart is boundless.

35. When in doubt, confused, impatient, loud, or selfish, these are important signs that the storyteller is very active.

36. When the student's mind is out of control, it creates illness. Fear is an illness, a disease, and sickness. Fear is not natural.

37. Prayers are not spoken nor answered in the storyteller. Prayers are answered in the heart. The storyteller must be quiet in order to hear the answer. Answers are given moment to moment. The heart never stops giving. Since this is the case, then once the questions stop, the truth will be revealed. A child may cry for its toy. After it stops crying, it looks around and sees toys surrounding it. The child never saw what it already had because it thought it had nothing.

38. The heart is joy. Joy comes with no attachments.

39. The heart is transparent; the storyteller hides till seen.

40. The heart learns in the experience of now; the storyteller doesn't trust now, so it just tries to recreate the same experience over and over. Not understanding all is new, now.

41. Unconditional love never stops growing.

42. Remove all conditions and the heart will show you what is.

43. Stop dreaming so awakening can happen.

44. To be awake is not to sleep, to sleep is to dream, to dream is to be conditioned.

45. There is no road to the heart; the heart is the road.

46. The flow of the heart is light. Light fills the mind, when the heart lights the mind, then words will express from a loving place for all.

47. The storyteller suggests a path, road, journey, or conditions to be a certain way before one can move correctly. The heart only knows now.

48. Wisdom is in the heart; intelligence is in the student's mind.

49. Heart is equality.

50. Love is translated by the storyteller as an idea, image, picture, story, or cult, but once it is understood then love can really flourish.

51. Possibility exists now.

52. Heart generated is strong, fast, and involves no time. Storyteller is slow, weak, and impulsive.

53. Listen with the heart and not the ears.

54. See with the heart and not the eyes.

55. Belief is a construct of time and mind. Belief does not exist in the heart.

56. Connect your heart with nature and she will guide you.

57. Breath, rhythm, mind, and heart should always move as one. When this happens all that is unlike the one will crumble in its wake.

58. Karma is made in the storyteller. Karma is simply not being loving. Forgiveness breaks karma through the heart. When forgiveness is heartfelt, then karma is done.

59. You cannot fake knowledge of the heart.

# PART 3

## The Book Of Innocence

1.   Innocence is the wonderment of life.

2.   With innocence comes playfulness and joy.

3.   Innocence is pure and purity is found where it has always been, right now.

4.   The search, seeking, reading, questioning, and road stops here. It is when the world out there is finally released to the inner world. And all at once everything is one.

5.   Both feminine and masculine exist here. Not as duality but synchronicity.

6.   Like a child curious of the next breath is where innocence flourishes.

7.   Nature is the guide, heart is the brain, and being is alive.

8.   Innocence celebrates laughter and playfulness because it knows that everything is coming and going, and it is useless to hold on to anything, or anybody.

9.   Innocence is awake but not as a final outcome of the mind but as the realization of now.

10.  All things, which were a constant reminder, fall away in the beauty of this grace. Grace is innocence.

11.  All prayers are answered here.

12.  Thinking about things, memories, attachments, have dropped away.

13. Innocence is a channel for the presence. All great work, ideas, artists, come from innocence.

14. Tomorrow, yesterday are past, so there is no more running to or away from anything.

15. Innocence is awareness, awareness is observing, observing is natural.

16. Innocence is compassionate understanding.

17. If you are thinking about this and wondering if you are innocent, or finding yourself comparing, competing, then perhaps now would be the time to put this down and walk in nature.

18. Nature is innocence.

19. Love is innocent, unburdened by yesterday, unburdened by the world, and unburdened by judgments of self.

20. Purity is innocent. Just like water is the pure, gasoline of the body temple, purity is the energy of love.

21. Purity is dropping heaviness of energy.

22. Talking about it, judging your self, and others will not allow it to be, because it is already here.

23. As discovered in Part 1 and 2, silence is nothing and nothing exists without investment. When you invest in love, which is enough, you will see nothing is lacking at all. When you invest in fixing, repairing, changing, and resisting, which are acceptable behaviors in the world, then you exist in

debt. Debt is to invest in lack. When you lack attention in the present, then you are indebted. If you invest in only now, then you invest in opportunities. Opportunities are only found now.

24. A child is innocent till made to feel guilty.

25. Right now you may feel guilty or in shame about what was, what will be, but remember that all is seen and unseen. How can an innocent child be guilty? When it has done nothing wrong.

26. Innocence is alarmingly simple. But since the investment is being made in tomorrow, then the energy of now is lacking. It is as though you keep taking gas out of the car and asking yourself, "Why doesn't the car run?" If you keep the gas in the car, then you will be able to move moment to moment without being scared of your own creation. God didn't create fear. So where does this fear exist, other then in a place that doesn't exist. So is fear a belief in a creation that doesn't exist? If it is, then by putting attention on a place that doesn't exist, the place will go away. When the place goes away then it can't be real, it can't be the truth. Correct. And yet the focus is on this place all the time.

27. Innocence is awareness.

28. There is nothing that exists that hasn't existed until attention is put on it. When attention is put on the real, all else goes away.

29. A child plays in the sand box. The child creates a game with other children. They make up rules, they make the game up, and then they create again. The game is always playful and

fun and it includes everyone. Does your games include everyone? Or are they excluded?

30.   Innocence is freedom to play and learn, nothing more. No right or wrong.

31.   Innocence uses the word sorry to delete the messages of the unreal. Sorry is a suggestion to yourself and others that you were simply not being loving in that moment. Sorry is not a punishment, sorry is not making your self right, and the other wrong, sorry is the simple awareness that we are one, and for a brief moment it was forgotten.

32.   Innocence acknowledges selfless living.

33.   There is no judge or jury even if someone lies to you, in innocence one does not hold on to it and punish the person. The innocent one understands where the lie came from. Forgives and moves on.

34.   Purity has no grudges for another, for it knows the other as it self.

35.   A tree stands strong in the ground; it moves with the wind, and losses its leaves continuously. New leaves replace the old and this is natural. Things come and things go. Life is innocent.

36.   Again please be reminded that if innocence is an idea or image in your mind then you are missing the point.

37.   You cannot act innocent, pure, and find it.

38.   Animals are innocent and people are too. Punishment for

our selves comes from not loving. The student punishes it self for doing cruel things. Withholding love from yourself and others is an act of punishment, and that is cruel. That is unnatural.

39.  Children ask questions from curiosity, which is innocence.

# PART 4

## The Book of Play

1. Playfulness is the foundation of the unlimited.

2. Laughter and tears come from play. When playing in life, love is activated.

3. Play and pray are one movement.

4. Play and love are one.

5. Play and life are one.

6. Play is the complete acceptance of now.

7. Play uses intuition as its guide and intuition is heart awareness.

8. Heart awareness is found before the labels of what is not happening.

9. Labels are restricting to play. Judgment is restricting to play. Gossip, condemning, eye for an eye is restricting to play.

10. Control of another through any means is restricting to play.

11. Play is wholeness. Play allows the other to be as they are without judgment of how they should be now.

12. Play is not a concept of mind.

13. Playing doesn't harm yourself or others. If it does harm you or others in any way then what you are doing is not playful.

14. Playing has one rule: Includes everyone.

15. Play does not exclude another, not even yourself.

16. Play invokes creativity.

17. Play has no drama, chaos those come from resistance.

18. Play is a celebration of now.

19. There is no competition or comparing in games.

20. Playing is caring. Caring is kindness. Kindness is selfless. Selfless knows the heart as the one.

21. Playing is appreciation of wholeness, that all is well.

22. Playing is not doing just to do. Playing has no sense of keeping busy as a form of impressing others.

23. Playing in joy.

24. Playing invigorates and uplifts naturally.

25. The mind plays games. The heart does not.

26. Play loves silence.

27. Play loves to love.

28. Play hugs naturally without wanting anything.

29. Play wants nothing, demands nothing, expects nothing, and embraces everything as it is.

30. Play responds to the action of now. Play responds with

justice for all.

31. Play is freedom.

32. Play helps and serves but doesn't save others.

33. Play is wonderful.

34. Play listens.

35. Play understands that all must be let go.

36. Play is healthy- it loves to exercise.

37. Sex is playful and should be shared from selflessness, not selfishness.

38. Play lets people go.

39. Play laughs and cries to heal when it is holding on.

40. Play is now.

41. Now is play.

42. Play is the high of the universe.

43. Play has created everything.

44. From nothing back to nothing is the joke of the universe.

45. Universe is always joking and playing.

46. The only thing you can be is a good listener of the heart.

47.   The mind is not a good play friend.

48.   The heart is a wonderful friend and guide.

49.   Playing is perfection of the one.

50.   Kissing Playfully is the intuition of the heart's response to joy. So intuition is gentle kisses from the universe. Enjoy the kisses.

# PART 5

## The Book of Stillness

1.  Stillness is Aum.

2.  The vibration of life is stillness.

3.  In stillness all can be seen, imagined, and known.

4.  In stillness the talk subsides and all is known and shared.

5.  Talking is labels, this book is nonsense, but in stillness it makes sense.

6.  Noise is the distraction of the unaware.

7.  Bring it all to stillness and it will be seen for what it is.

8.  Stillness allows the truth that is personal to break away and become impersonal.

9.  Stillness is equality.

10. Stillness understands stillness.

11. In stillness there is no end.

12. Stillness reveals that all is growing and revealing moment to moment, and that the moment is not fragmented by anything.

13. Be Still.

14. Still Be.

15. Awareness is stillness and nature itself is.

16.  Confusion, doubt, trouble, are thoughts that seem to create problems, and yet there is no problems.

17.  Realized is the acceptance of the real.

18.  Reality is not a thought, idea, and image.

19.  Stillness reveals the one.

20.  All is one and all is still.

21.  Thoughts are distractions from the real. The real takes effort to understand. You may discover when ever. You may not. You may decide that you don't want to know who you really are. Wonderful.

22.  Stillness relies on nothing because it is everything.

23.  In stillness the idea of death is an idea.

24.  In stillness everything is seen as entertainment from itself. The moment the idea that is created from stillness is called its own, then it is no longer the original idea, it becomes dead. The moment the idea is acknowledge from where it came, then the idea is shared with everyone and will be abundant.

25.  Selfishness is not found in stillness; therefore all is created from beyond intellect.

26.  Wisdom is found in the heart and the heart is found in stillness. Stillness is found in nothing. Nothing is found in everything. But when everything is found then nothing is found. Hence the paradox of the whole.

27. Stillness loses everything to become nothing. This is what scares the mind, for the mind wants something, because it thinks.

28. Smile.

29. Finding it in the mind will not help you. Go to the place where it is and the discovery of the absurd will fall away.

30. There is no perfect life that is not already perfect.

31. Remember the light created all as it self. In stillness this will be sensed.

32. The mind is sand and the heart is foundation.

33. Simply be aware, change nothing, see everything from the heart.

34. There are no secrets, nothing can be hid from you, and all is transparent.

35. A disciple is disciplined in staying in the real.

36. We are all disciples of either the real or unreal.

37. There is nothing to fight since there is nothing to fight.

38. Observe your inner fight to see the outer fight.

39. Do not believe these words, do not follow, but instead discover for yourself if this book is true.

40. Do not turn this into a cult, religion, or knowledge, but tune into it.

41. Welcome home sweet friend.

# PART 6

## The Lost Book Of Light: The Origin

1.  There is only light. We are light. This is the truth, foundation, and beginning of everything.

2.  Light emanates from one source.

3.  It has no division and so it cannot be divided.

4.  The source of the light is immense. It is everywhere and in all places at once.

5.  There is no place the light is not.

6.  So as a light, each is whole, perfect, complete, and constantly radiating this fullness.

7.  Each light expresses it's own uniqueness.

8.  Any disconnection from the light is based on the experience of the false appearing real, like a dream.

9.  Light observed a sound, then discovered through sight where the sound came from, next came a strange smell, then came the sensation of air, Then it observed touching this thing outside of itself. Then it observed through these senses that it had a body of its own; it felt panic, trapped, and that is when a thought came, "I".

10. Other lights started forming bodies and sounds. The sounds were used to communicate simple things. Getting use to the body was interesting. First the legs wouldn't work, so crawling was very effective. Once crawling was used then walking on two legs became the next step. Lights were amazed by the body and by their arms, the senses, and by the vast land. Discovering this land was fun and fun to do

with others. You could make up games. Games at first were simple, communication was simple, and so the rules were simple. They found it fun to entertain each other.

11. When the lights began to notice their bodies were different the lights began to "think" about those differences. It started to lose the silence through "thinking". But each light was unique and they began to confuse the body and mind as who they were.

12. The stories that were told were scary in nature, to grab the attention, and keep them entertained. They talked of conflicts, wars, battles, revenge, and hate, which the light knows nothing about. But it used its imagination. First stories were created by sound, then sound became words, words became language, and so forth. Hence the story is the lie. Stories can be good or bad. A story can be misinterpreted, but always there must be division. Light, remember has no division.

13. Light likes to play games with it self. Other lights get together and talk about other lights as though they were different in some way.

14. When light created this body and mind- silence was the birthplace. Light is charged up by its source through silence and quiet.

15. This last statement is not an idea or image.

16. Noise is the nature of the unnatural. Stillness is natural.

17. At this point in the process called the slowing down.

18. The light gets caught up in what it is seeing, more than listening to the silence. Getting caught up is called phenomenon.

19. Human came to the light, which means God man.

20. So light feeling lost, abandoned, and indifferent to the other objects it was seeing created a story of this place. The story was created to help it feel safe again. After it created the body known as a suit to experience earth mother. The story came from the unexamined question, "Why am I scared to be one?"

21. The light created a being called God. I suggest being, because most lights still believe God is a man/woman. And when you create a story you need a villain, and that villain was called the devil. Lights recognized that all good stories need a villain to keep it going.

22. It is here that groups formed to talk about this God who must be somewhere. Since they were caught in the phenomenon. They believed in what they saw (Thought) rather than what was real. This created competition and comparison. Everything was outside and inside became lost. If you feel scared now reading this, please go back to 4.

23. This period seemed like a forgetting. The first lie in the story is to forget that you are light and connected to all. When one forgets who they are, they create a story to identify with. They tell the story over and over, to keep the identity going. But it is a story of a false self. Light needs nothing to be light. A story is the suggestion that one is not already light.

24. In the period of forgetting began stories about God. As the

lights forgot who they were they projected this on the image of God. Making the suggestion that God had forgotten them, because they forgot themselves.

25. The division continued. Fake knowledge came about: fake knowledge to "know" what was known in silence.

26. Since the sun captivated them, they were mesmerized when it would leave and darkness came, they believed that this God was bad at night and good in the day. The lie began to grow. The second lie, which states that there is darkness and light existing at the same time.

27. So stories were created upon stories about a God who would punish you. The lights felt like they were being punished; punishment happens when self-love is forgotten.

28. Now the God had division. There was dark and light. They labeled the dark bad. How could they not, they didn't understand it? They called the light good. Just terms, just words, for darkness didn't really exist. But it was so real, that it felt like it did. It felt real by the continued story of what wasn't.

29. Others began to tell stories of the dark light. The dark light only came at night. But when it came it was scary. Sometimes the dark light was called darkness.

30. So at night the lights would tell stories about dark light. It had to be a devil and be different then this God. This God must be against the dark light. Again the light was getting caught up in its own creation. Not realizing that the fight was never with another but was within.

31. So the stories went. And there was division among the light.

32. God and the devil fought. And yet they both were made out of nothing.

33. Remember there is only light and light comes from one source. In case you are getting caught up in the story right now.

34. The third lie came, the period of will.

35. During this period the stories got out of hand. Now there was good light and dark light. The good was caught up fighting the bad. Each one began to form groups and tell stories about the others. If you liked the stories they told in a group, you would join that group. If you didn't like the stories of the group you would form a story about that group and join the other group.

36. Now a funny thing happened: people began to feel safe, secure, and happy in their groups. Judgment made them feel safe. It kept them from accepting. In each group they formed groups of people who they entrusted to create more safety and security. These groups within the groups felt more secure then the others and created rules to keep everyone happy. Everyone wanted to be happy. Nobody liked to fight. But they were fighting both inside and out.

37. One-day dark light and good light met wills. The third lie called will is based on the story that you are granted will over another person, over your life, and that no-body could stop you. When in actuality to be willful is to simple express your uniqueness and let others express theirs. But the story had grown too much. They were discussing expansion in

their groups. The groups had become too big and willful for the space they inhabited. It was at this meeting that the two different stories from the two different groups became confused. They were no longer hearing each other. They went back to their groups and told them that the other side wouldn't let them be free with more space. That it was their free will to do, as they wanted with space. They motivated the groups and as the light forgot and became more willful, both dark and good, began to learn ways to punish the others. Like the story of God and the devil, forgetting the truth that there was nothing against them.

38. The good said the others were like the devil and claimed they were working for the good of God. The dark said the same about the good.

39. And when the sun and the night met, which was called dusk, the two met. Confused by willful stories about each other, they refused to let go and forgot that light cannot defeat light. They played a weird game called war.

40. This was marked as a frightening time. Something strange came over them. It comes over every light before it fights another. The shadow. Although some lights didn't like it, others on both sides loved it. They felt like they could do anything they wanted to the other. They were possessed by will.

41. At dusk some lights began to cry. It didn't like the frightening time. By then the war had begun forgetting more of what it already was. But this time the war was outside not inside. Both inside and outside were one. The story of the wills became truth. Told over and over. What was real? What was not? This would later be the breaking point.

42. These bodies during the war seemed to bleed, break, and be very sensitive to punching.

43. After a period marked in space, these bodies laid everywhere. Bloody, broken, hurt, and yet, the most unusual event happened.

44. There were bodies that seemed to have no light in them anymore. There were just these shells that looked like the person had looked. The fourth lie was named death.

45. This period of death was strange to the lights. Some became really sad. Others didn't want to look, looked away, and others became even more caught up in the story of them that did it. Some found silence again, because the noise didn't make sense anymore.

46. One light sat in the darkness with its eyes closed and found answers in the silence. When the sun came up, the light knew.

47. What did the light know?

48. The light talked of a place called home, A place where all was one and together.

49. That challenged all the stories that had been told.

50. Other lights were confused. And yet others came to listen to the truth.

51. Another story was beginning to grow about this light that discovered home and was healing people.

52. Some hated this light, "Who does this light think it is?"

53. Death had become time. Time had become thought and thought was noise.

54. The light spoke of the timeless.

55. The light instructed them "do not follow me", but instead go there yourself and experience it.

56. But others needed a road map. Their stories were novels now. They were lost, confused, but in light still.

57. The light instructed them that dark and good don't exist in the one.

58. Each of you is the one.

59. Others didn't want to hear the truth anymore. Their stories they read daily and this story made no sense in comparison to one they were reading. And because it made no sense they decided to end this light. They formulated rules to stop the spread of this light. If it spoke again, then they would have to punish it. These groups of lights were living a story of power, greed, ownership, and couldn't see anymore. They were blind to the light.

60. The one light again spoke of the one and the oneness and all of us as a community.

61. The powerful story of "having/getting more" told by dark light couldn't take it anymore; they had formed groups around the land called religions, political systems, organizations, and businesses, more power, control, and stories.

Some groups were loved for this strange power over others. They even created a thing called money to control the group. The game was played out. Lights of all kinds found value in money. They realized if you had more money then you had more power, and could do what you wanted. The group called this valuing your self. You could value more light with more money. All would love you. They forgot again money was simply the effect not the cause.

62.  That story enticed so many lights that they believed that with this money they could be safe. They could build their own castles, boundaries, prisons, and pay others to watch their possessions. They craved power.

63.  From there systems called banks and government were formed. They came and made up rules and more rules on getting more of this money from other lights. They got money through paid labor, and taxes. They also created stocks, loans, credit, and other things to keep the light from seeing that it was connected to the whole. Thus began lack.

64.  And yet other lights began to connect to this thing called home. There were no rules, only acceptance, and from there came one voice. That voice was different then the powerful, and oppressive voices. That voice came to unite and not divide; it responded with care rather than reaction and punishment as had become the norm.

65.  Other lights that were developing this one voice were becoming powerful. They weren't seen in the media, but they met in circles of light. They celebrated, danced, united, created, loved, and sang about the one light.

66.  The oppressive lights didn't like this at all. So they began to

create more weapons, armies, and police, to end the celebration of light. "STOP IT", they shouted. But remember there is only light and light is all there is.

67. Other lights didn't like this. But the media reported daily about war, battles, death, destruction, famine, and poverty. "Where is this unity?" politicians laughed and degraded. They wanted to remind the world of the lie story, and keep the lights separated.

68. It seemed overwhelming, Crazy, and confusing, "How could this be? What happened? Nothing was making sense anymore."

69. Other lights began to say, "Turn off the media they are corrupting. They are not showing the truth." Lie number five, the truth. This truth became personal. What seemed like good advice still added to the oppressions of the world.

70. And yet, young lights were being birthed throughout the land. They were pure and began to raise the light back home. Much older lights were beginning to remember the story wasn't real, and remembered the place called home.

71. As in many stories told over the timelessness of the vast abyss called light, there comes one final fight. The fight to let go of the story and accept the place called home. As light would leave bodies, it would come back into different shells and experience itself in a new way. In this new way the light would learn how to come back home correctly, and live from itself again.

72. During this time of the final fight many, many lights had decided to come back into the shells to celebrate, create,

dance, and sing as one again. Like they did eons ago. These lights have come from many different universes to party.

73. It is and will be a party as never experienced before. The stories will be wiped off the map and money will be meaningless in trade.

74. Communities will form, equality will be all there is, and service to all will be easy.

75. The light will no longer create money, religion, politics, organizations, and business that separate people; it will take care of mother earth and replenish her while celebrating the feminine and the masculine as one. Not as a story, but as light.

76. Lights will plant, create and celebrate with family, friends and communities.

77. Life will light and light will be life.

78. When the light leaves the shell. The shell will feed and nourish the land. The shell will be celebrated for the light it carried. Not the story of the shell mind.

79. The communities will teach each other how to plant, make homes, cook, take care of the land, and connect to silence to recharge.

80. Nature will rule, teach, and educate the children.

81. Purpose will come from listening to the silence and adding to the planet.

82. Yoga, Tai Chi, qigong, energy work, and meditation will be learned by the children and practiced by all.

83. Dawn and dusk will be used to meditate and connect to silence.

84. Light will be as it always has been.

85. All stories will be left in books.

86. As the light shines back on the land without division, the land will be as one.

87. Solar energy and power will be all that will be used on this land.

88. It is happening now.

89. Is happening now.

90. Light to light.

91. You are light.

92. Light comes from one source.

**Still unfolding...**

# Acknowledgments

O-Books and Moon books: Thank you John Hunt, Mary Flatt, Nick Welch, Stuart Davies, Trevor Greenfield, and Catherine Harris.

Jules Anne Bruff for being my second eyes and guiding me early on this process.

Harper Soleil Brown my sunshine, my moon, my life, and my daughter who is such a blessing.

Support Group: John Gloria, Eric, Sofia, and Rose Werner, Pat and Dave Brown, Korena, Phoenix, Carlo Novoa, Charlotte Ciralo, Kathleen and Charles, Vincent, Angelina, and Ra Ra, the Telucci's, Brown's, Emmanuel Dagher, Brian Walton, Karen Brailsford, Sacred Circle, Teachers, Carl Speigelberg, Harvey and Danny Berman, Rose Jabbour, Ed Trujillo, Todd Stockwell, Success Brannon, Unity Church of Burbank, Westside Unity, Unity Antelope Valley, Steve Allen, Kelly and Dana, Gini Gentry, Robert Taylor, and Agape International Spiritual Center, UTSLA, and my many clients, audiences that I spoken in front of as well. Anyone I have left off, my apologies.

# DAVID MATTHEW BROWN

David is an internationally sought after spiritual motivator on Universal Principle. David is also an author, teacher, Metaphysician trained at AGAPE International Spiritual Center, and former radio host of INSIDE OUT where he dialogued with over 362 guests. Including: Swami Kriyananda, Archbishop Desmond Tutu, Don Miguel Ruiz, Marianne Williamson, Byron Katie, Dr. Bernie Siegel, Cynthia James, and Matthew Fox. He hosted and reported at Dr. Jane Goodall's DAY OF PEACE, where he interviewed top celebrities on peace, including Pierce Brosnan, Soleil Moon Frye, Marilu Henner, and Rose Byrne. David has been consulted as an expert on TV and Radio. He speaks on rotation at Unity Burbank, Westside Unity, and Unity Antelope Valley. David has one on one session's with clients, which he calls "the work". The work is a mixture of modalities, which help the client break through their story and to live an inspired and empowered life.

To contact David for speaking or to have a session with David email: semjase64@gmail.com

# BOOKS

O is a symbol of the world, of oneness and unity. In different cultures it also means the "eye," symbolizing knowledge and insight. We aim to publish books that are accessible, constructive and that challenge accepted opinion, both that of academia and the "moral majority."

Our books are available in all good English language bookstores worldwide. If you don't see the book on the shelves ask the bookstore to order it for you, quoting the ISBN number and title. Alternatively you can order online (all major online retail sites carry our titles) or contact the distributor in the relevant country, listed on the copyright page.

See our website **www.o-books.net** for a full list of over 500 titles, growing by 100 a year.

And tune in to myspiritradio.com for our book review radio show, hosted by June-Elleni Laine, where you can listen to the authors discussing their books.